Divinity in Disguise

*Nested Meditations
to Delight the Mind
and Awaken the Soul*

KEVIN ANDERSON

CLB PRESS

ISBN: 0-9728355-0-4

PRINTED IN THE UNITED STATES OF AMERICA
AT PHOENIX COLOR, HAGERSTOWN, MD

In loving memory of
Robert James Anderson
(1925-2002)

The death of a dear friend, wife, brother, lover, which seemed noth-
ing but privation, somewhat later assumes the aspect of a guide or a
genius; for it commonly operates revolutions in our way of life, ter-
minates an epoch of infancy or of youth which was waiting to be
closed, breaks up a wonted occupation . . . or a style of living, and
allows the formation of new ones more friendly to the growth of
character.

Ralph Waldo Emerson

TABLE OF CONTENTS

The Sacred Other

Obstacle Illusions

Livelihood

Joy

Acknowledgments

All the people who have inspired me as a writer and influenced me on the path of spiritual growth are hidden between the lines of these pages.

This book was written in the several months after my father's death. Aside from whatever value this work may offer the world, it has already served its purpose by reenergizing my spirit after that first intimate encounter with loss.

When I began writing, I knew this book would be dedicated to Dad, yet I intended to keep him within the margins of the dedication page. At that goal I have failed, and thankfully so.

Robert James Anderson is present in these pages in two ways. First, because the writing took place so soon after his passing, a number of the pieces reflect the loss and subsequent spiritual transformation that his death brought about in my life. Second, his lifelong love of wordplay is an integral component of the nested meditation form. Growing up with a man who was always searching for double meanings was the perfect training ground for this form of writing. His enjoyment of wordplay was evident until the end. The morning a physician told him that putting a shunt in near his liver would kill him, Dad responded, "Then we shunt not do that!"

Near the end, he told us that he prayed his death would bring healing to each of his loved ones in whatever way she or he needed. For my part, Dad, your prayer has been answered. This book is a tribute to your enduring spirit.

I express deep gratitude to Claudia for being my wife, soul companion, family co-creator, and friend. Without her steady support this book would never have come to light. Likewise, I thank our children (Sarah, Emily, Jessica, Elisabeth, and Jim) for listening to many of the pieces contained in this volume and offering their enthusiasm. Their presence in my life is pure grace.

My parents, Bob and Mary Jo Anderson, created a family environment which was my first experience of Divinity in disguise. They taught me that life is sacred and that God's presence enfolds us in every moment, during both joyful and difficult times.

Each of my siblings has been a gift to me in his or her own way. Bob, Rick, Gerry, Ruth, Judy, Joan, Christy—I am honored and privileged to share the path through this life with each of you. Additional thanks to Bob and Judy for their remarkable support during the time that I was wrestling with the angels.

Jim Anderson stood with me unwaveringly while I was making the difficult transition to a fuller embrace of life and of other creative pursuits. The time, hope, wisdom, and humor he so freely gave have been crucial to my growth as a person and to the publication of this work.

John Florian has been a soul friend and companion through all of my adult years. The friendship we share has been one of the great gifts of my life. He was the first to deem me a "poet" and has taught me the power of affirmation and claiming one's gifts.

I offer thanks to Dean Ludwig and Jim Rataczak who, by their courage to live the artist's life as they have imagined it, have emboldened me to do the same.

Several others have offered the gifts of friendship, encouragement, and challenge. These include Chuck Thayer, Mark Davis, Ann Welly, Jim Devine, John Graden, Pat Corrigan, Mark Nafziger, and Bill Anderson.

As my editor, Judy Ludwig contributed numerous hours and ideas that improved the book, and her great enthusiam for the project helped me believe in it. She gave freely of her encyclopedic knowledge of commas and other grammatical mysteries. Pauline Glaza led me gently into the foreign world of computer layout. Her expertise and encouragement were greatly appreciated.

May all of the people who have graced my life know that they are Divinity in disguise.

INTRODUCTION

In this book a new form of written expression is introduced. I call these pieces meditations rather than poems because they are at odds in several ways with what is considered poetry today. These meditations are presented in a layered or "nested" format. They reveal themselves one line at a time, with each stanza containing the previous one, much like a set of Russian matryoshka dolls. A fuller description of this nested form is available in the appendix for interested readers.

While the goal of these meditations is to awaken a sense of the sacred in the ordinary, this is not a book that focuses only on the joyful aspects of being human. Grace is to be found in joy and sorrow, birth and death, love and loss, faith and doubt, and the many other polarities of existence. The reader who is looking for a collection of exclusively positive, "inspirational" pieces will find some of these meditations too dark. I have not attempted a calculated balancing of light and dark pieces. Because this book was written at a time of personal transformation and grappling with the reality of death, these and related themes appear in many of the pieces.

Books of poetry generally allow the poems to hang on the pages like paintings on a museum wall, with no accompanying commentary. *Divinity in Disguise*, however, includes quotations and prose reflections. This is in keeping with the overall purpose of the book, which is to offer the reader a diverse reflective experience rather than simply a collection of poetic writings.

How to Experience a Nested Meditation

Because this form of writing is new, I offer five guidelines for how to fully experience a nested meditation.

First, these pieces are most richly appreciated when read aloud. As a meditation shifts direction, some of the new meanings can be carried by voice tone changes. Sometimes sentences switch from declarations to questions (or vice versa) or pause in new places; it is the reader's inflection that conveys these nuances.

Second, the repetition built into these pieces is intended to give them a meditative quality and to allow each stanza the possibility of delivering meanings distinct from the others. Some readers may be tempted to skip the repetition of earlier lines to more quickly discover what the final stanza has in store. This approach will miss some of the richness of this form, for most of the meditations have multiple meanings. The final stanza, which includes all the earlier lines, does not contain the whole meaning of the piece. There is no requirement that all the stanzas harmonize or point in the same direction. Sometimes they actually point in opposite directions, emphasizing the often paradoxical nature of truth.

Third, when read aloud, the meditative nature of these pieces can be enhanced by pausing for at least a full, slow breath cycle (one inhalation, one exhalation) between stanzas. This allows each stanza to soak in as its own distinct meditation before moving on to the next. If the pieces are read aloud as part of a group meditation experience, they can be paced even more slowly to allow for intervening periods of silent breath work.

Fourth, once an entire piece has been read, earlier stanzas may appear in a new light. Circling back may reveal new opportunities for reflection.

Finally, as the teacher in the movie *Dead Poets Society* told his students, feel free to rip these pages out of the book and experience the meditations however you choose! May this new form of written expression, juxtaposed with the words and ideas of others who have made the human journey, stir in you an awareness of what Abraham Joshua Heschel called "the inconceivable surprise of living."

Wellspring

I saw a tree bowing down.

I saw a tree bowing down
and asked: "Do you do God's will?"

I saw a tree bowing down
and asked: "Do you do God's will?"
It whispered, "I do."

I saw a tree bowing down
and asked: "Do you do God's will?"
It whispered, "I do
God's willow."

I like trees because they seem more resigned to the way they have to live than other things do.

Willa Cather

Walking up the driveway to get the newspaper about a month after my father died, I saw the willow with the broken branch. The ice storm that hit the day we buried Dad had torn up the trees in much the same way his death had ripped me open. I was learning that just when you think you're fine, grief can ambush you. The sight of a broken branch in a willow tree can leave you kneeling in the driveway sobbing.

This was the same willow that years earlier had served our daughter Emily and me as a place of reconciliation. We had been planting the garden one spring morning when tension came between us because I was continually telling her that the seeds wouldn't germinate well if she kept covering them over with large clods of dirt. I couldn't see that I was heaping large clods of criticism on *her* germinating spirit.

When she had heard enough, Emily stomped off and climbed the willow in the front yard. I was close to commanding her to come down from the tree when I decided to climb it and talk with her instead.

There, among the slowly swaying branches of the willow, Emily and I had a heart-to-heart and eventually returned to plant the rest of the seeds.

17

I've glimpsed God.

I've glimpsed God,
though not looking down.

I've glimpsed God,
though not looking down
as a Divinity in the skies.

I've glimpsed God,
though not looking down
as a Divinity in the skies,
but hidden all around and within.

I've glimpsed God,
though not looking down
as a Divinity in the skies,
but hidden all around and within
full view—a Divinity in disguise.

Every human being is a divinity in disguise.

Ralph Waldo Emerson

During the years I was growing up, my father would spend hours looking out the picture window at birds. I couldn't imagine what the fascination was. At some point I probably decided it was just something of interest to old people.

When I was thirty-five, Dad asked me to go bird-watching with him during the spring migration. I agreed, thinking I'd at least get some time with him, even if I experienced the birds as little more than boredom in plumage. I was amazed to discover what all birders know—that there is an exquisite pleasure in beholding in the circular view of binoculars a creature you've never seen before.

The next spring, while walking in the woods behind our home, I saw a hooded warbler for the first time. This splash of brilliant yellow, wearing what appears to be a black executioner's hood, startled me with its beauty. After that encounter I wrote a poem, the first two lines of which are: *I saw God in the woods today / in a hooded warbler's guise.*

Now I get it, Dad. To paraphrase Emerson, you knew all along that even birds reveal Divinity in disguise.

God is in the details.

Ludwig Mies van der Rohe

I'm a star!

I'm a star,
white-of-the-eyes white, brilliant!

I'm a star,
white-of-the-eyes white, brilliant,
but a pinhead.

I'm a star,
white-of-the-eyes white, brilliant,
but a pinhead-
sized hole in the universal mask.

I'm a star,
white-of-the-eyes white, brilliant,
but a pinhead-
sized hole in the universal mask
concealing the face of God.

This world we live in is but thickened light.

Ralph Waldo Emerson

Emerson's intriguing "thickened light" metaphor brought to mind the first weeks after Uncle Dick suffered a stroke. Complications during surgery on a carotid artery had left my mother's brother paralyzed on one side. He couldn't eat or swallow properly. Everything they gave him at the rehabilitation center had to be thickened. Even the coffee was thickened. Though it had real coffee in it and even a coffee flavor, it was more like pudding than coffee. "Drinking" it was only remotely like the experience of drinking coffee should be.

I often feel the same way about trying to take in this world. God is everywhere in evidence around us, but we usually see the Divine as if through thickened light that distorts our perception. We get glimpses—a starlit night, intimate time with a loved one, the release of a belly laugh—yet we long to see God face to face.

Perhaps God's face *is* looking back at us from all of creation, or from behind the eyes of loved ones, or the eyes of strangers, or the eyes we see when we look in the mirror.

My love for you is limited.

My love for you is limited
by nothing.

My love for you is limited
by nothing
less than a longing for the perfect lover.

My love for you is limited
by nothing
less than a longing for the Perfect Lover
who conceived us both.

Men and women cease to interest us
when we find their limitations.

Ralph Waldo Emerson

During the early phases of courtship, our beloved may appear radiant—a perfect match for all of our needs. In time, we are disillusioned to learn that our lover is not perfect. We discover that we have projected our desire for the perfect lover onto our partner, who looked for a time as if she or he could play the part.

The longing we feel for the perfect lover is one with the longing for God. Psalm 62 stated this truth thousands of years ago: "My soul rests in God alone." The 12th-century poet Rumi wrote about how our connection to God is in our longing for God, much like the connection of a dog to its master is in the dog's whining for the master.

In human relationships there is no such thing as unconditional love. We feel the potential for such love in the deep connections we experience with our spouses, children, or other loved ones, but we cannot offer them totally selfless love. Only God loves with such perfection.

Until I am essentially united with God,
I can never have full rest or real happiness.

Julian of Norwich

Reveal yourself.

Reveal yourself,
my God, my Lover!

Reveal yourself,
my God! My Lover,
I am waiting, I am naked always!

Reveal yourself,
my God! *My lover,*
I am waiting, I am naked always
beneath all that veils the now.

I have seen what you want; it is there, a Beloved of infinite tenderness.

St. Catherine of Siena
(translated by Daniel Ladinsky)

Every man or woman on this earth walks around naked all the time, just beneath his or her clothes. The difference between "dressed-to-the-nines" and "in the buff" is about one-eighth of an inch or less, depending on the fabric you're wearing. God is naked everywhere too, just beneath the layers of busyness and preoccupation that shield our view.

It should not be surprising that mystics through the ages have spoken of God as a lover. In the vulnerability and intimacy of human passion, we get a hint of the ecstatic union with our Maker we sense is our ultimate destiny. Deeply spiritual women and men also have an unusual ability to see God revealed in the routine moments of life.

Much of the time we are like the adults in *The Emperor's New Clothes*, unable to see what is obvious to a child. Rare are the occasions when we simply put our minds in neutral and experience the present moment disrobed of regret about the past or anxiety about the future. The only moment in which joy and peace can be ours is *now*, Eckhart Tolle teaches in *The Power of Now*. The truth of this simple yet challenging insight is immediately apparent.

Much of seeing God revealed in the present moment involves first accepting *now* as it is. In labeling *now* as boring, mundane, unproductive, or intolerable, we throw more and heavier garments over the divine Reality beneath reality. Then we wonder why God is so hard to see in our lives.

No one can stay aware of the present moment all the time, but that is where God waits for us—"a Beloved of infinite tenderness."

What's sacred?

What's sacred
is concealed.

What's sacred
is concealed
like a salamander by a stone.

What's sacred
is concealed
like a salamander by a stone
at the edge of the narrow stream.

What's sacred
is concealed
like a salamander by a stone
at the edge of the narrow stream
of your awareness.

Everything in nature contains all the power of nature.
Everything is made of hidden stuff.

Ralph Waldo Emerson

Great Smoky Mountain National Park in Tennessee is known as the salamander capital of the world. Even so, it takes a bit of work to find these creatures. When we camped along the Little River in the Smoky Mountains, our then five-year-old daughter Elisabeth spent hours looking for them. "I found another one!" she would scream with joy each time she made a new discovery.

I didn't find a single salamander during the whole two-week trip. That's because I didn't have the patience to go along the edge of the stream turning over rocks the way Lizzie did. She knew that if she kept turning over rocks, she'd eventually be rewarded with the thrill of finding a new orange or black or spotted salamander.

The sacred is everywhere in full view. When we cannot see or feel it, it is we who have concealed it from ourselves, we who place the rocks and we who fail to overturn them. Preoccupations narrow our awareness and push the sacred to the edge of the stream of our consciousness. But, oh the joy that awaits when we return to the wondering perspective of a five-year-old!

Fertilize the ground.

Fertilize the ground
of your being.

Fertilize the ground
of your being
with soul manure, real fresh.

Fertilize the ground
of your being
with soul manure—real, fresh
experience of mundane things.

I've worn hip waders twice in my life. Once was fishing for wall-eye with my brother Rick. The other was standing nearly waste high in a mixture of cow manure and urine in the back of a dump truck.

Dad loved chrysanthemums, so one year he decided to plant a large plot of them in our back yard. He was into organic before organic was a buzzword, so the only fertilizer he considered for the mums was cow manure.

I remember showing up at the farmer's barn with an old dump truck. That manure redefined the meaning of the word "fresh." It hadn't even had time to dry out and thicken, so we found ourselves shoveling a dark slurry of nitrogen-rich dung into the truck.

The mums were spectacular. A local gardening center was pleased to purchase them from us. Much more pleased, I'd say, than all the neighbors who lived downwind.

The best place to seek God is in a garden.
You can dig for him there.

George Bernard Shaw

God is.

God is
the Eternal Head!

God is
the eternal head-
water of every stream.

God is.
The eternal head-
water of every stream
of consciousness flows in.

God is.
The eternal head-
water of every stream
of consciousness flows in
the heart of every moment.

God is.
The eternal head-
water of every stream
of consciousness flows in
the heart of every moment
I immerse myself in deep awareness.

We are a stream whose source is hidden.
Our being is descending into us from we know not whence.

Ralph Waldo Emerson

When we took the Maiden of the Mist boat ride at Niagara Falls, I wasn't sure if it would be the sort of tourist activity that we normally try to avoid. You know the kind—where you pay a lot of money and come away underwhelmed. We learned that the boat ride is, in fact, a spectacular way to see the falls.

The American falls are picturesque enough, but when we slipped into the horseshoe of the Canadian falls, it was as if we had sailed into the mouth of God. From the river, we looked up through clouds of mist to behold 700,000 gallons of water per second streaming down. That's a lot of outpouring, and to think that it's been flowing that way nonstop for thousands of years! I've come to regard Niagara Falls as nature's visible model of how God invisibly pours energy into creation in every instant of time.

Did you ever wake up at 3 a.m. and hear your heart beating in the silence and wonder who or what is keeping that vital muscle going? There is indeed a life force descending into us in every moment from, as Emerson would say, we know not whence.

The Sacred Self

Find still water.

Find still water
in any storm by going deep.

Find still water
in any storm by going deep
beneath the surface tumult.

Find still water
in any storm by going deep.
Beneath the surface tumult,
the sacred self dances like seaweed.

Be still and know that I am God.

Psalm 46:11

A friend, John Florian, has a knack for posing interesting questions. There we were, driving along in the foothills of the Appalachian Mountains in eastern Kentucky. It was our yearly retreat on which we spend three days together talking about life, fatherhood, women, and work between golf and tennis matches and plenty of guitar playing. Out of the blue he asks: "If you were a member of a Native American tribe and the chief were to give you a name to signify your essence—your primary gift to the tribal community—what would the name be?"

Within thirty seconds I came up with a name, but it was for him. "You I will call Morning Sky," I announced. He liked the name and it has stuck. It took only a minute longer for us to come up with a name for me.

Morning Sky and I e-mail each other almost daily. He addresses his letters to "Still Water," a name which captures both who I am and the sacred self for whom I search when I feel more like "White Water."

If we go down into ourselves
we find that we possess exactly what we desire.

Simone Weil

The rain came while we slept.

The rain came. While we slept,
the placid stream became a white wall of fury.

The rain came. While we slept,
the placid stream became a white wall of fury
at the ancient boulders for refusing to give.

The rain came. While we slept,
the placid stream became a white wall of fury
at the ancient boulders for refusing to give
up their sacred places.

If you visit Great Smoky Mountain National Park in the off season, you can get a campsite right on the Little River, a gorgeous mountain stream strewn with boulders. We'd had good weather for ten days before an all-night downpour transformed the Little River into a wall of white water passing uncomfortably close to our camper. Most of the rocks that had been visible the day before were now under water. Only the largest boulders protruded above the torrent, and as the raging water slammed into them, it sprayed high into the crisp morning air. Yet the boulders held their sacred places.

That scene has become a metaphor for me of what it is like to attempt to live a soulful life in a culture that bombards us daily with messages that would have us deny our spiritual selves. Refusing to allow oneself to be washed away by busyness, pursuit of material gain, or preoccupation with youth or beauty is to become a boulder of spiritual courage in the torrent of secular culture.

To be nobody-but-myself—in a world which is doing its best, night and day, to make you everybody else—means to fight the hardest battle which any human being can fight, and never stop fighting.

e.e. cummings

I have plans to retire.

I have plans to retire
from working so hard.

I have plans to retire
from working so hard
at being someone.

I have plans to retire
from working so hard
at being someone
else.

Being true to oneself is the law of God.
Trying to be true to oneself is the law of human beings.

Confucius

"My Dad just retired. He's been looking forward to doing all the fishing he's put off for years because of his busy professional life."

I was talking to the man's daughter. Her father was several feet away—in a coffin. She was still speaking in the present tense, as the recently bereaved often do.

Many of us have ideas of who we'd like to be someday, of lives we dream of leading in the future, yet we keep focused on the culturally-prescribed goal of "being someone."

Pondering recently how we are prone to say "no" to possibilities by flowing with the stream of conformity, the following meditation came to me:

> No, no, no
> no, no, no, no,
> no, no, no, no—Yes!
> Know, know, know, know. . .

Once you make a decision,
the universe conspires to make it happen.

Ralph Waldo Emerson

I could never hold a candle.

I could never hold a candle
to your life.

I could never hold a candle
to your life,
but I will do my best.

I could never hold a candle
to your life,
but I will do my best
to hold my own.

I couldn't even hold a candle as an altar boy! I remember walking up the center aisle of Little Flower Church at 6:00 a.m., half asleep and holding the processional candle too close to my chest, suddenly smelling the pungent odor of burning hair. That's when I first learned about setting myself ablaze for the greater glory of God!

When my father died, I was surprised to find in the mix with all the emotions of grieving a sense of deep inadequacy, a feeling that my life could never measure up to his. He had touched so many lives with his humor, generosity, intellect, and spiritual searching that I simply felt my life could never radiate as brightly as his had. Then I realized I didn't have to shine like he did. I just need to shine like I do.

My thanks to our daughter Jessica, who came up with the last line of this meditation during one of our pre-bedtime snuggles. In the ambiguity of that line, she captured the tension we sometimes feel between trying to hold our own against standards outside of ourselves and simply focusing on holding our own candles up to shine, regardless of how they compare to the lights of others.

You are the light of the world.

Jesus of Nazareth

My father never filled his father's shoes.

My father never filled his father's shoes,
and I have never filled my father's.

My father never filled his father's shoes,
and I have never filled my father's.
May you, beloved son, be the one!

My father never filled his father's shoes,
and I have never filled my father's.
May you, beloved son, be the one
who never fills mine!

Is the parent better than the child into whom he has cast his ripened being? Whence, then, this worship of the past?

Ralph Waldo Emerson

One morning when our son Jim was just over a year old, not long after he'd learned to walk, I saw him standing in my size thirteen basketball shoes attempting to make his way around the kitchen. The shoes were on the wrong feet and, being hightops, came up nearly to his knees. He wasn't getting anywhere too easily, given the awkwardness of the fit. Long after snapping his photograph that morning, the image of Jim standing there trying to fill my shoes lingered.

My feet are long and narrow. Jim has the wide feet that come from Claudia's side of the family. His feet will probably be too wide someday to fit into my shoes. I hope his spirit is too.

An oak is the dream every acorn has.

An oak is the dream. Every acorn has
to let go and fall.

An oak is the dream. Every acorn has
to let go, and fall
is the time.

An oak is the dream. Every acorn has
to let go and fall.
Is the time
close for you?

*The greatest achievements were at first and for a time, dreams.
The oak sleeps in the acorn.*

James Allen

The sacred self knows that, like acorns, the fullness of our being is realized only after we let go. But, oh, how we hang on!

One of the many things my parents had no idea I was into as a young boy was acorn fights. My neighborhood friends and I often would climb oak trees, stuff our pockets with acorns, and hurl them at each other. I remember once when the opposing team ran out of acorns, climbed down their tree, and began throwing *rocks* at my friend Dan and me. Realizing the danger of the situation, we began hurrying down the tree. When the dead branch I'd placed my foot on broke, I fell about thirty feet to the ground. (The distance gets a bit longer each time I retell the story!) All the way down, my bare arms scraped on the bark. Luckily, there was a bush at the base of the tree that cushioned the fall. I remember being proud of the bloody wounds I showed the others as I emerged from the woods.

Unfortunately, in adult life it's rarely clear when we fall—unexpectedly or by choice—where we will land or whether there will be anything to soften the impact when we hit ground. A range of emotions from exuberance to raw fear may whirl in us as we let go and allow the oak to begin its awakening in our lives. And we don't tend to show our wounds or be proud of them.

I am becoming.

I am becoming
a diamond in the rough.

I am becoming
a diamond in the rough-
est part of my life.

I am becoming
a diamond. In the rough-
est part of my life,
the pressures are just intense!

I am becoming
a diamond. In the rough-
est part of my life,
the pressures are just intense
enough to form a jewel.

The kingdom of heaven is like a merchant searching for fine pearls. When he finds a pearl of great price, he goes and sells all he has and buys it.

Jesus of Nazareth

Dean Ludwig, my brother-in-law, makes museum-quality rocking chairs. Each one is a handcrafted work of art. Each also has a price tag that could knock you off your rocker! I was standing at Dean's booth at an art fair when I heard the following conversation between a young couple:

> Man: That's the most beautiful rocking chair I've ever seen!
> Woman: Yeah, and it costs more than our car did!

Wisdom is a lot like that rocking chair. Most of us would like to have it, but we're not exactly lining up to pay the price.

And what is the cost of that jewel of great price we call wisdom? Not three thousand, not even three million dollars—just three *decisions*: the *decision* to give ourselves fully to all the joy and pain that come with loving others deeply; the *decision* to make our lives more about spiritual growth than growth in our bankrolls or our egos; and the *decision* to focus our existence on a higher purpose, a noble mission that allows us to give away what suffering and joy have taught us about soulful living.

Who will grant the permission I seek?

Who will grant the permission I seek
to live the life I have?

Who will grant the permission I seek
to live the life I have
for so long imagined?

Who will grant the permission I seek
to live the life I have
for so long imagined
others have?

Who will grant the permission I seek
to live the life I have
for so long imagined?
Others have
chosen to stop seeking.

Who will grant the permission I seek
to live the life I have
for so long imagined?
Others have
chosen to stop seeking
permission.

I have learned this at least by my experiment: that if one advances confidently in the direction of his dreams, and endeavors to live the life which he has imagined, he will meet with a success unexpected in common hours.

Henry David Thoreau

In *The Heart Aroused*, David Whyte addresses the ancient tension in the human soul between the pursuit of security and the desire to live one's deepest longings. "Who will grant the permission I seek?" attempts to capture the tension of which Whyte speaks: the way it feels to live in a culture which so often seems to conspire against creating an authentic existence. Are we simply to accept the life we have? Are we to risk the life we have for the life we imagine and long for? How do we deal with the constant materialistic urgings of the culture that would have us measure our worth more by the square footage of our houses than by the expanse of our own inner space?

We may believe we are living the life we have imagined, but sometimes that's because we haven't allowed ourselves to imagine much outside of the culture's prescriptions. If we do allow ourselves to feel the longing for a more soulful life, we experience a holy unrest, a divine discontent that is known to all seekers.

The Sacred Other

We are all one.

We are all one
step from the edge.

We are all one
step from the edge
of the annihilation.

We are all one
step from the edge
of the annihilation
of all hatred.

I consider myself a Hindu, Christian, Muslim, Jew, Buddhist, and Confucian.

Mohandas Gandhi

The great problem with organized religions throughout recorded time has been the tendency for followers of each tradition to believe that their view of truth is the right one. This illusion that we are separate groups of people seeking different gods has led to many shameful chapters in human history. When political beliefs are held with such zeal, the results are similar, as occurred during the Cold War.

Growing up, I often felt afraid of nuclear war. For a time after the Cold War, I felt that fear slipping away, but September 11, 2001 changed that. Now it seems as if any day holds the potential for horrific news. The temptation with terrorism is to think that getting rid of terrorists will solve the problem. "The line dividing good and evil," said Alexander Solshenitsyn, "cuts through the heart of every human being." If we want to annihilate hatred, we must first conduct a search and destroy mission within ourselves.

He had the uneasy manner of a man who is not among his own kind, and who has not seen enough of the world to feel that all people are in some sense his own kind.

Willa Cather

We buried her in the woods.

We buried her in the woods,
then, in amazement, heard our daughter's voice.

We buried her in the woods,
then, in amazement, heard our daughter's voice
ask if we could let her go.

We buried her in the woods,
then, in amazement, heard our daughter's voice
ask if we could let her go
forgive the dogs that killed her cat.

*We must make our homes centers of compassion
and forgive endlessly.*

Mother Teresa

On a lazy Sunday afternoon several years ago, our children first experienced how life can blindside routine existence with grief. A neighbor rang the doorbell and told us that her huskies had just mauled our cat, Princess. After holding and consoling the children for two hours, Claudia and I made our way back to the woods with them for a service. There, after returning Princess to the earth, we encircled the grave and said a tearful prayer. On the way back to the house, Elisabeth, then four, uttered the question that inspired "We buried her in the woods."

Even the death of a cat has the power to remind us that life is fragile. If huskies can maul our cat on a lazy Sunday afternoon, what could this world do to our children? Small events suggest the possibility of larger ones.

When faced with senseless tragedy, adults—blinded by prejudice, fear, and greed—are more likely to say, "Let's go kill the people who killed our people" than to seek reconciliation. The world's response to unprovoked violence is more violence. If taken to heart by every person on the planet, the wisdom in Lizzie's question could bring about the lasting peace for which humans have yearned throughout history.

I honor you.

I honor you,
my soul.

I honor you,
my soul
companion, as you are.

I honor you,
my soul
companion, as you are
Divinity in disguise.

. . . to honor and love all the days of my life . . .

Traditional marriage vow

"Love" may be the most overused word in the English language (with the possible exception of "like" as used by, like, a lot of teens). How often, though, do we think about what it means to "honor" another person?

Honoring someone means treating him or her as one deserving of great respect. Honoring starts with ourselves. A person who is highly self-critical will be critical of others as well. Someone who is self-honoring is more likely to honor others too. Honoring another begins with accepting a person "as is." Paradoxically, when we honor another person with acceptance, we free her or him to grow and change.

Today we hear a lot about "soul mate" relationships. I prefer the term "soul companion" because "soul mate" implies a perfect match, and there is no perfect lover for any of us but God. Yet a love marked by deep honoring throughout a life spent together is perhaps the surest way to unmask the great Love, alive in us all, that conceived the world.

Wet are the strokes of life.

Wet are the strokes of life
upon you, a still being.

Wet are the strokes of life
upon you, a still-being-
painted masterpiece.

Wet are the strokes of life
upon you, a still-being-
painted masterpiece
God is calling "Claudia."

The Toledo Museum of Art owns two paintings by Vincent van Gogh. "The Wheat Field" draws me to it each time I stroll through the gallery. Van Gogh used such thick paint that it is raised off the surface of the canvas, giving a three-dimensional effect to his work. The heavy paint almost looks as if it is still wet, even though van Gogh hasn't painted anything for over 110 years.

This meditation was first written for my wife, my love, Claudia. I have since made it a gift to several other people I cherish simply by changing the name in the last line.

In this life we are all unfinished masterpieces. Every one of us, you might say, is all wet. And a gracious, mysterious Artist, the same one who never tires of painting sunrises and sunsets, is calling us each by name.

Never lose an opportunity of seeing anything that is beautiful; for beauty is God's handwriting—a wayside sacrament. Welcome it in every fair face, in every fair sky, in every fair flower and thank God for it as a cup of blessing.

Ralph Waldo Emerson

I picked you.

I picked you
to be my wife.

I picked you
to be my wife
and I didn't know you.

I picked you
to be my wife
and I didn't know you
were a wildflower.

I am not at all the sort of person you and I took me for.

Jane Welsh Carlyle

"I picked you" is one of Claudia's favorite nested pieces. It sat framed on her bedside table for a few years before I shared my interpretation of the circular nature of it. By "circular" I mean that after reading the final line, one loops back to the first line and finds a different meaning. There is no way to avoid the reality that those we love most in life are also those we hurt most easily and frequently. Fortunately, there is a way in committed love of being reconnected to our roots after we've been picked. It's called forgiveness.

The third stanza of this piece expresses a great truth about marriage. We promise our lives to another person, thinking we know him or her, yet time reveals to us how much was unknown. If marriage were a real estate transaction, every sale would be "as is" and without a complete list of disclosures.

The years teach much which the days never knew.

Ralph Waldo Emerson

Make love.

Make love
a gift exchange.

Make love
a gift. Exchange
desire for delight.

Make love
a gift. Exchange
desire for delight-
ing the love of your life.

The manner of giving is worth more than the gift.

Pierre Corneille

Anyone who experienced the 1960's might expect the second stanza of this piece to be: Make love, / not war. In reality, there is a subtle war that occurs in bedrooms all over the world, a civil strife that burns in the hearts of men and women and is stoked by what fuels all wars: an inability to see beauty in difference.

Women often feel men are deficient in helping create the emotional intimacy that makes sexual love a celebration of closeness. Men, who have about forty times more testosterone than women coursing through their bodies, often feel women are deficient in sexual desire. Sometimes the conflict burns in the open; other times it is a smoldering resentment or an icy withdrawal that signifies a resignation that the other will never really understand one's sexuality.

Developing a sacred sexuality requires more than a truce on this private battleground. It involves making love a gift exchange. Christmas is magical to children in part because of the anticipation they feel wondering if they'll receive the gifts they most desire. As we grow older, however, the excitement of giving a gift that has been made or selected with great care far surpasses the anticipation of receiving. Likewise, when we focus on delighting a partner the way she or he most enjoys being delighted—when the sensual is an extension of other-centered love instead of a demand to meet one's own needs— intimate and erotic energies suffuse the whole relationship in an ongoing gift exchange.

Do your wife.

Do your wife
a favor.

Do your wife
a favor
and caress her.

Do your wife
a favor
and caress her
mind and spirit.

Do your wife
a favor
and caress her
mind and spirit
before you ask, "Tonight?"

I remember Dad giving me the sex talk a few years after I had experienced the initial shock of learning the truth about how each of us got here. Nothing in his Catholic background had prepared him to do a good job with the talk, and it was, bless his soul, pretty pathetic. I think he asked if I knew what a couple of slang words meant and then told me to just remember that sex is a sacred thing. The whole talk lasted less than five minutes.

But he was right to call it sacred. Anything that reveals the mysterious and powerful *Reality behind the reality* of our lives is sacred. Sex can do that, if we can get past the shallow messages about it that abound in advertising and the media.

Part of the reason that women and men do not experience sexuality as sacred more often is that their experiences of sexuality are frequently so different. Men seem programmed to celebrate sex at a moment's notice, regardless of the current emotional climate of the relationship. Women are more likely to experience sex as sacred only when the relationship feels emotionally and spiritually intimate. Both approaches are valid. What's crucial is an ongoing attempt to understand and honor the other person's sexuality.

If the sacred isn't to be found in the act that creates life, I'm not sure where it would be found.

The world is charged with the grandeur of God.

Gerard Manley Hopkins

Our children drank like hummingbirds.

Our children drank like hummingbirds
from the flowering of our passion then.

Our children drank like hummingbirds
from the flowering of our passion, then
hovered for a moment.

Our children drank like hummingbirds
from the flowering of our passion, then
hovered for a moment
and were gone.

What a moment it was lying there on the floor with our two youngest daughters pressing their ears against my chest as I sang "I Shall Not Be Moved" in the deepest tones I could muster! They wanted to hear the sound directly through my chest wall without the intervening distortion of air, so each had a finger stoppering her other ear.

That night I dreamt about hummingbirds. If you've ever had a hummingbird feeder, you've witnessed how these creatures can hover nearly motionless for a few seconds while drinking, then abruptly disappear a moment later. (Sometimes, like children, they're back sooner than you think they will be!)

Some moments in the raising of children are so holy, so unmasking of divine grace, that there is a nostalgia that sets in almost immediately, an awareness that the moment is now a part of family history and can never be recreated in exactly the same way. But what a delicious nostalgia that is!

A little work, a little sleep, a little love and it's all over.

Mary Roberts Rinehart

Every day I lay my heart down.

Every day I lay my heart down
on the parent's gamble.

Every day I lay my heart down
on the parent's gamble
for the pure gift of your being.

Every day I lay my heart down
on the parent's gamble:
For the pure gift of your being
in my life, I risk the pure dread of losing you.

Making the decision to have a child—it's momentous. It is to decide forever to have your heart go walking around outside your body.

Elizabeth Stone

Before Claudia and I had children, I never knew how much fear lies in the shadows behind the radiant love a parent feels for a child. This fear became intensified in me after working as a psychologist with several families who had lost children in tragic ways. Having seen up close how wrenching the loss of a child is, just putting our children on the bus in the morning seemed like a gamble.

The first visit I ever made to a casino was in Atlantic City. It took me about an hour to work up the courage to put a first bet down on the blackjack table. The minimum wager was five dollars, and that was a lot more than I wanted to risk. I ended up having a pretty good run and had enough sense to walk away before I lost it all.

Every day we all—parents or not, adults or children—bet the whole stack of chips we call our lives. This life, however, is a casino with one rule: No matter how much you win, you can't leave until you lose it all. And the truth is, we don't know how or when we are going to die or lose our loved ones. This reality makes celebrating the Divine in our lives—disguised as a spouse, a child, a sibling, a parent, or a friend—a matter that cannot wait for tomorrow.

Listen to your children.

Listen to your children
tell you how they see.

Listen to your children
tell you how they see
deep into your self.

Listen to your children
tell you how they see
deep into your self-
begotten blindness.

When I passed through the dark wood of my early forties, I spent a year so disoriented that I became completely blinded to my own worth. Because of serious health problems and the sense of broken-ness that accompanied them, my previously successful career as a psy-chologist was falling apart. I was learning the hard truth about what Wayne Dyer wrote in *Your Sacred Self:* "If you are what you do, then when you don't, you aren't." During the same period, my father was suffering from a mysterious illness that would eventually take him from us. Life, which until then had been going quite smoothly, sud-denly felt frightening.

Among the people who reached out to me during that time were our children. Sarah painted me a candle illuminating the darkness, and she posted KTYADL ("Know That You Are Deeply Loved") signs in hidden locations all over the house. When I told Emily that I sometimes felt too soft, too vulnerable for the world, she said, "Dad, *gold* is soft!" Jessica offered comfort in the form of a snuggle with me every night before her bedtime. Lizzie remembered me nightly dur-ing the mealtime prayer. Jim, at three, simply radiated hope and acceptance.

We expect ourselves to be our children's teachers, yet we are wise to let them be ours as well. When I was blind, our children were faithful seeing-eye dogs who helped me find my way until I could see my own beauty again.

You yourself, as much as anybody in the entire Universe, deserve your love and affection.

Buddha

A father fertilizes.

A father fertilizes
the Godseed in each of his children.

A father fertilizes
the Godseed in each of his children
by letting them know him as he is.

A father fertilizes
the Godseed in each of his children
by letting them know him as he is
growing into his own.

A friend I made while cooking for a volunteer program in Kentucky later moved to my home town and became a friend of my parents. When I met John, I almost missed the Divinity in him because half of his vocabulary consisted of four-letter words! I had been raised to consider foul language a serious stain on one's character, even though Dad often used milder versions of it when he was angry.

John told me that Dad would frequently loosen up around him, getting past his "I have to be a role model for my children" mode. In John's presence, Dad could enjoy being crude without looking over his shoulder. Never before I was thirty-five, and only rarely after, did Dad let me see that part of him uncensored, just as it was.

During my "dark night of the soul," our children saw me as I was. There was simply no way to hide it. But they saw me, too, as I was growing into a more authentic self. Perhaps that time will provide fertile ground for them to realize that sometimes an intense and destructive blaze is just what is needed to awaken the Divine seed in us.

The seed of God is in us. Given an intelligent and hardworking farmer and a diligent field hand, it will thrive and grow up to God, whose seed it is; and accordingly its fruits will be God-nature. Pear seeds grow into pear trees, nut seeds into nut trees, and God seed into God.

Meister Eckhart
(translated by R. B. Blakney)

Obstacle Illusions

Don't ask poison questions.

Don't ask poison questions
such as, "Why can't I be more like you?"

Don't ask poison questions
such as, "Why can't I be more like you
and how soon?"

Don't ask poison questions
such as, "Why can't I be more like you?"
and, "How soon
can you be more like me?"

Humans are comparing creatures.

M. Scott Peck

We poison our spirits when we constantly tell ourselves that we should be more like somebody else. When we put ourselves down for not being as talented or attractive or successful as other people, we block the flow of divine energy through our own unrepeatable combination of gifts.

Likewise, we poison others' spirits when we demand that they be more like us. Most married people fall into the trap of thinking they can change their spouses. Parents often attempt to mold their children to a predetermined end rather than nurture the Godseed in them. When we demand that loved ones change to fit our needs, we are really expressing the longing for God, the one with whom we will fit exactly.

Several years ago, I wrote a song called "St. Peter's Question." It draws on the traditional Christian image of meeting St. Peter at the gates of heaven after death. The chorus of the song is:

> The toughest question I expect to face
> when I make my way to the gates of heaven
> isn't, "Why weren't you more like somebody else?"
> but, "Why weren't you more like Kevin?"

I saw myself.

I saw myself
down like a tree.

I saw myself
down like a tree
and wonder why.

I saw myself
down like a tree
and wonder why
I feel so stumped.

I have offended God and humankind because my work did not reach the quality it should have.

Leonardo da Vinci

My life has been nothing but a failure.

Claude Monet

If I'm in the company of da Vinci and Monet, I suppose I won't criticize myself for criticizing myself. But I will try to be more vigilant for that harsh voice. I call it "the heckler," a name I chose after watching a clown in the dunking booth at a local fair. He was an expert at heckling the passersby into laying down their money for three chances to put him in the water. Such a knack he had for hitting people in their weak spots! I was strolling by and minding my own business when he called out, "Hey, you bearded sissy!" How did he know I was the one in the family who cried more than boys are supposed to?

On the third throw I put him down, but he climbed right back onto his perch, chanting, "High and dry, high and dry!" and scanning the crowd for the next person to heckle.

As long as we stand in our own way, everything seems to be in our way.

Ralph Waldo Emerson

I'm getting older.

I'm getting older
ways of thinking.

I'm getting older
ways of thinking
out of my life.

I'm getting older
ways of thinking
out. Of my life
plans, none calls for self-criticism.

I celebrate myself, and sing myself.

Walt Whitman

I remember sitting curled up like a frightened possum in a corner of my room while one of my older brothers and his friend teased me about not being able to sing anything, not even "Row, Row, Row Your Boat." I was ten and I had no idea that someday I would enjoy writing, singing, and performing songs immensely.

Whether we are vocalists or not, our main task in being alive is to celebrate and sing ourselves to the world. To some, this "singing myself" idea sounds selfish, but I think it is no moreso than a flower blossoming to add its beauty to a lush garden. We cannot blossom or find the rhythm and melody of our lives, however, when shame and self-criticism keep us curled up in a corner.

Trying to live with constant self-criticism is like attempting to sing after breathing helium. You could probably still manage a few notes, but you'd sound more like a munchkin in the *Wizard of Oz* than yourself! Dump self-criticism like sandbags off a hot air balloon. Your spirit will soar, your life will sing!

My wife is my home.

My wife is my home
improvement project.

My wife, is my home
improvement project
raising you up?

My wife, is my home
improvement project
razing you? Up-
holding our oneness must be two.

My wife, is my home
improvement project
razing you? Up-
holding our oneness must be two
pillars of acceptance.

Recently I installed a window for the first time in my life. Fortunately, it was for a pole barn, not anything that needed to be just right. The installation was a comedy of errors. My collection of tools was severely lacking. The handsaw I was using was rusty and bent. The dog kept running off with my work gloves and protective goggles and chewing them up. While cutting through the metal siding of the barn, I fell off the ladder and sliced my finger on the sharp edge of the metal. By the time the window was secured, it was not quite level or square, and I found myself hoping that no one I knew would ever inspect the job up close.

That's about how it goes when I try home improvements on Claudia. With the wisdom of nearly twenty years of marriage, I'm learning that it's best to forgive her for not being God, the Perfect Lover. Anyone who tries to force a spouse to change, ends up with either a counterfeit partner trying to appear to be who the other wants, or a resentful person who digs in her or his heels as a way of holding onto an authentic self.

Everything in life that we really accept undergoes a change.
Katherine Mansfield

I'm doing too much.

I'm doing too much
time in the prison.

I'm doing too much
time in the prison
of my self.

I'm doing too much
time in the prison
of my self-
elected busyness.

Business! I think that there is nothing, not even crime, more opposed to poetry, to philosophy, ay, to life itself, than this incessant business!

Henry David Thoreau

The assumption that life is inherently busy is endemic in our society. Many people live with a sense of time famine but do not realize that it is their own way of relating to time that creates the shortage and the hunger. Time is the very stuff of our lives, and how we use it is a continuous exercise in priority setting. When we say, "I know that's important, but I just don't have time," we're really saying that, for now at least, other things are more important to us.

Recently my sister Judy, a mother of six, told me that her life feels "full, but not busy." Leading a *full* life means we have many purposeful activities on which we choose to spend our time. Being *busy* means feeling overwhelmed by too many activities that we don't perceive to be of our own choosing.

We imprison ourselves when we assume that our time is not really our own. We can escape that confinement by remembering that, in continually making choices about priorities, we hold the keys to a richer and more satisfying way to live.

Help me!

Help me,
damn it all!

Help me
dam it all
up awhile.

Help me
dam it all
up awhile,
the rushing!

Help me
dam it all
up awhile,
the rushing
river of time.

My life is not this steeply sloping hour,
in which you see me hurrying.

Rainer Maria Rilke
(translated by Robert Bly)

A few summers ago I rode a roller coaster, The Raptor, in the seat next to our daughter Jessica. After acting brave the entire time we waited in line, Jessica began screaming on the way up the big hill: "I'm scared! I'm scared! I want to get off!" It was too late, of course—we were strapped in for the duration. During the ride she continued to yell comforting things such as, "I'm slipping out of my seat!" The pull-down harness over my head and shoulders was so constricting that all I could do was reach over with my hand to feel for her leg to determine if she was still there.

Some days as a mother or a father make you feel you've floated down the river of your single life, taken the plunge over the waterfall of marriage and parenthood, and found yourself caught in the undertow of family and work pressures, waiting for something called retirement to spit you out and let you float peacefully away again. But retiring will be just re-tiring if we don't become practiced now at realizing that we are the only ones who know where the controls are that can slow the flow of time. It takes courage, instead of reaching for loved ones in the churning foam, to make the decisions that allow time to flow more like a peaceful river than a ride on The Raptor.

You don't see me.

You don't see me
like I am.

You don't see me
like I am
you.

You don't see me
like I am.
You
see me like you are.

Read the meditation below carefully several times:

You and I
are swimming like fish in the
the ocean of our nonconscious ideologies.

Did you catch the repetition of "the" at the end of the second line and the beginning of the third line? Many people miss this because our brains do not give us absolute reality; rather, they feed us an edited interpretation of absolute reality.

Did you ever wonder why a three-way light-bulb seems to get much brighter when it goes from 50 to 100 watts, but only slightly brighter when it goes from 100 to 150 watts? The change in brightness is the same in both cases (50 watts). Our brains, however, register not the actual change, but the *percent* change in brightness. (Fifty to 100 watts is a 100% change, while 100 to 150 watts is a 50% change.) Our brain plays tricks on us—and not just with light-bulbs.

What is a nonconscious ideology? It is a deeply ingrained way of looking at life that deludes us into thinking our worldview is reality. Thinking, for instance, that life is about accumulating material things is a nonconscious ideology—an illusion that can invisibly shape the choices we make and the way we live.

The wisest fish in the ocean are those that periodically jump out of the water and wonder what all the wet, wavy stuff is below.

Everyone takes the limits of his own vision for the limits of the world.
Arthur Schopenhuaer

Livelihood

Work is a prayer.

Work is a prayer
for the day's end.

Work is a prayer
for the day's end
or until the day's end.

Work is a prayer
for the day's end
or until the day's end,
and we choose which.

Your work is to discover your work
and then with all your heart to give yourself to it.

Buddha

My father's father often said that he considered work to be a prayer. My siblings and I were raised with the same message, but as a boy I generally found work to just be work.

Many people think of work as just something that must be done to pay the bills or attain a higher standard of living. We often cannot see the choices we have for creating a life worth living because our culture continuously leads us to believe that work is about making money, advancing, and acquiring things rather than about expressing one's gifts in prayerful service to the world.

Most of us find the responsibility of creating an authentic existence—which includes choosing work that allows us to express our essence in meaningful service—to be too daunting. In his book, *Escape from Freedom*, Erich Fromm described how we dodge the responsibility of creating authentic lives by conforming to what everyone else is doing and convincing ourselves that we have no choice.

Perhaps my favorite of my father's aphorisms is: "Any life worth living is worth living differently." By leaving a secure job with the family business in order to pursue research on sustainable agriculture, Dad made the last twenty years of his working life a prayer for the future of the earth.

Work is our livelihood.

Work—is our livelihood
worth what it costs?

Work—is our livelihood
worth what it costs
us in time?

Work—is our livelihood
worth what it costs
us? In time
we will know.

A good friend once told me that as his career progressed, he was continually faced with choices between making more money or preserving time for himself and his family. "I've made the best decisions when I've chosen time over money," he told me as we sipped red wine by the fire.

The majority of people in the world are both time- and money-poor. They live an existence marked by the daily struggle for survival. Others not caught in material poverty choose to make the pursuit of money primary in their lives. Often they end up living with a sense of time famine and troubled, time-starved relationships.

When those of us who have our basic needs met continue to choose money over time, we run a high risk of impoverishing our personal lives. If we consistently prioritize time over money, however, we open up a whole new world of possibilities for our lives and our relationships. We can become intentional about living by creating a deeper, countercultural vision of love and by investing time in moving toward that vision. Instead of allowing work to get the best of us, we could decide to let our spouses, families, and friends get the best of us. Or perhaps we could commit ourselves to the ideal of living with balance so that both our work and our relationships prosper.

Make your work to be in keeping with your purpose.

Leonardo da Vinci

I am doing so well.

I am doing so well
for myself.

I am doing so well
for myself
I am leaving you.

I am doing so well
for myself
I am leaving you,
my God, speechless.

Character is that which can do without success.

Ralph Waldo Emerson

Much is revealed about the soul of our culture in the common expressions we use. "He's doing well for himself," we say, or "She's made a big name for herself." The individualism and focus on wealth in our society result in a spiritual poverty. Many of us are so busy trying to do well for ourselves that we pay little attention to doing well for others beyond our immediate loved ones. We may volunteer time occasionally or give money to charity, but the primary preoccupation of our waking lives remains getting ahead.

Ask yourself the following questions: Do I have the character to do without success as the world defines it? Do I keep my life uncluttered enough to hear a call to a deeper way to live? Is my way of living leaving God speechless?

As one whose spirituality is anchored in the Christian tradition, I find it helpful to remind myself frequently that Jesus was an unemployed drifter who owned nothing, bummed shelter and food off of others, and was put to death as a common criminal. He didn't do well for himself, but he did quite well for others.

Be a leader.

Be a leader
where you are.

Be a leader
where you are
most needed as one.

Be a leader
where you are
most needed as one
who germinates the Godseed in others.

Be who you are where you are.

St. Francis de Sales

What is leadership? In a word, service. When Christ walked the earth, people kept trying to put a power label on him ("King"), but he insisted on leading by serving.

We often think of service as giving time or money to the materially less fortunate, as if only they need to be served. But the spiritually poor in our culture vastly outnumber the physically poor. People are starving for models of how to live soulfully.

Anyone who is about the task of discovering a spiritual, authentic way to live serves humankind by example. This kind of leadership, by women and men of all walks of life, is what the world needs most. By letting our true selves shine like the morning sun into our families, our communities, and the world, we awaken the best in others.

You must be the change you wish to see in the world.
Mohandas Gandhi

Compensation isn't just.

Compensation isn't just
money for time.

Compensation isn't just
money for time
we give the corporation.

Compensation isn't just
money for time.
We give the corporation
our very souls.

Money often costs too much.

Ralph Waldo Emerson

The cost of a thing is the amount of what I call life which is required to be exchanged for it, immediately or in the long run.

Henry David Thoreau

In *The Heart Aroused*, David Whyte wrote eloquently about the importance of keeping soulfulness alive in the workplace. Some employers get their workers to give the corporation their very souls in a dehumanizing sense. Many people trade their lives for financial survival or security, but their work does little to help them grow or develop as human beings. Other companies encourage their workers to give their souls in a humanizing way. These still unusual workplaces match the human need for purpose with a corporate culture that values employee growth as much as growth in market share or stock prices.

I remember asking a wealthy, middle-aged client what he did for a living. Without hesitation he said, "I'm a soul-seller." He described how his dedication to do whatever it took to make the next sale had reduced his personal life to an empty shell. A spiritual approach to work involves seeing it not so much as something one does to *make a living*, but as a key element of *making a life* that allows one to give the essence of his or her soul to the world.

I'm in stocks.

I'm in stocks
and bonds.

I'm in stocks
and bonds
since I've made big money.

I'm in stocks
and bonds
since I've made big money
my master.

MAMMON, n. The god of the world's leading religion.

Ambrose Bierce

Keeping a healthy attitude about money is one of life's perpetual challenges. We say that money can't buy happiness, but we find ourselves reading about the latest lotto winners with wonderment that the Greeks might have saved for humans made immortal by the gods.

In my life, as in psychological studies, money has not been correlated to well-being. At the times I've made the most money, I've found myself stressed by the responsibilities involved and unable to keep a consistent focus on what I considered most important. As I write this book, I am making less money than ever in my career, yet my spirit is filled with a sense of abundance and gratitude.

The tension between the desire to live with a deep sense of purpose and the desire to be secure materially has been part of the human condition for millennia. It's what that carpenter two thousand years ago was talking about when he said that no one can serve two masters.

Of course, money will do after its kind, and will steadily work to unspiritualize . . . the people on whom it was bequeathed.

Ralph Waldo Emerson

I fancy a simple life with no hunger.

I fancy a simple life with no hunger
for money or material things left.

I fancy a simple life with no hunger
for money or material things left
unfed.

I fancy a simple life with no hunger
for money or material things. Left
unfed,
my soul becomes voracious.

Remember this, that very little is needed to make a happy life.

Marcus Aurelius Antonius

My brother Gerry kept gerbils for a while when we were growing up. I remember the annoying squeak of the circular cage as those little rodents did their daily workouts.

Harvard professor Juliet Schor, author of *The Overworked American* and *The Overspent American*, says that millions of us live in the "squirrel cage of work and spend." We work hard for our money, spend too much of it, then need to work even more to satisfy the bill collectors and our ever-changing expectations about the standard of living we require to be happy. Once we reach a plateau, we look at others who have more and find ourselves back in the squirrel cage.

What a strange cycle! The more we make life about filling ourselves up with material things, the more our spirits hunger for meaning. Money and possessions are like diet soda—they satisfy momentarily, but they do not nourish. They are best seen as pieces of a broader plan to live with depth and purpose.

We need a redefinition of "quality of life" that emphasizes a livable pace, connected relationships, enriching leisure, and spiritual health over an unbalanced focus on material gain.

It is not the person who has little, but who desires more, that is poor.

Seneca

Take time to discover.

Take time to discover
what you are to do.

Take time to discover
what you are. To do
what you are is everything.

Take time to discover
what you are. To do
what you are is everything
you are to do.

People should not consider so much what they are to do,
as what they are.

Meister Eckhart

Recently, at a workshop I gave for ministers, I ran into a client I'd worked with years ago. When he first came to me for counseling, Michael was torn about what to do with his life. His path then was focused on becoming the kind of man he thought his father would respect. I remember vividly a dream he related about being atop a giant skyscraper, only to see his father on a slightly taller skyscraper next to him. In the dream, his mother was at the base of the buildings telling him it was O.K. to come down. As we worked together, it became clear that the true longing of Michael's soul was to become a minister, a direction he thought his father would never understand or respect. How delightful it was to see him years later representing his congregation at the workshop!

In *Do What You Are*, Paul Tieger and Barbara Barron-Tieger use a well-established personality test to determine the kind of work for which a person is most suited. When we put the question "Who am I?" ahead of "What kind of work shall I do?" we are likely to choose work that lines up with our natural passions. With this approach, work can be more than a job, more even than a career. It can become a calling to manifest our gifts to the world.

Brokenness

Life is breaking me.

Life is breaking me
like a bone.

Life is breaking me
like a bone
that long ago healed.

Life is breaking me
like a bone
that long ago healed
wrong.

To destroy is always the first step in any creation.

e.e. cummings

When I was a boy, my best friend broke his arm on three different occasions while playing with me. The first time he was chasing me with a stick and tripped. A few years later we were boxing, and his arm just snapped when his hand connected with my head. The third time I fell on him as we careened over what we called "Suicide Hill" while standing up on a toboggan. It's amazing that his mother allowed him to continue spending time with me.

I have never broken a bone, but I have experienced brokenness of the spirit. If I had to choose, I'd pick a hundred broken bones before experiencing such darkness again. I've come to see, however, that I was in a cocoon then, ready to let go of many of the limitations of my way of being in the world up to that point. A cocoon is a dark and confining place to weather the winter, but it is also a vessel of transformation.

Reading Wayne Dyer's *Your Sacred Self* helped me realize that both our joys and our sufferings are vehicles of Divine grace. Focusing exclusively on "the pursuit of happiness" leads us to deny pain or unrest in our souls. Sometimes our greatest leaps of growth come, as the poet Rainer Maria Rilke wrote, "by being defeated decisively."

Accept where you are.

Accept where you are
broken.

Accept where you are
broken
and let your spirit flow.

Accept where you are
broken
and let your spirit flow
through the cracks.

Ah! if you only knew the peace there is in accepted sorrow.

Jeanne de la Motte-Guyton

M. Scott Peck's famous first line from *The Road Less Traveled* — "Life is difficult"—probably sold a large percentage of the millions of copies of that book in print. But to those wise three words I would add, ". . . and we make it more difficult than it needs to be." By railing against our sufferings, by judging them as intolerable blockades to the happy life we seek, we miss the opportunity to experience the gift of brokenness. Difficult times can teach us how we help create our own suffering or how we can more completely understand the pain of others.

Acceptance is a great virtue. My first real awareness of this has come in letting go of my father—in simply accepting that he died a strange death years before I imagined him leaving us. Even as I write these words, the acceptance wavers, but the alternative is living angry at life and at God, which would lead only to the diminution of my spirit. Acceptance requires a willingness to let life be mysterious, to make friends with our finitude, to allow the Infinite to remain inexplicable, beyond our greatest efforts to piece together the puzzles of pain and loss.

I have fallen so far.

I have fallen so far,
and I feel rotten

I have fallen so far,
and I feel rotten
outside and frozen inside.

I have fallen so far,
and I feel rotten
outside and frozen inside
like an acorn beneath an April snow.

A one hundred acre parcel of virgin oak trees called Goll Woods is among the few remaining places in our part of the country where a person can see what trees were meant to be. In this sanctuary, trunks seven feet in diameter at the base shoot skyward like great pillars in a forest cathedral.

The first time we visited Goll Woods, the towering bur oaks inspired this poem:

> Witness
> the old bur oaks,
>
> what majesty comes of patience,
>
> what greatness ascends in time
> from every godseed left undisturbed,
>
> what lofty burdens are borne
> by simple rootedness and balance.

When we visited Goll Woods a year later, a storm had toppled about half of the stately trees. The woods looked like a battlefield; limbs and corpses of giants were scattered everywhere. What took hundreds of years to grow, nature destroyed in minutes. In several hundred more years, the results of that storm will be seen in the majesty of oaks that grew up only because an opening was made in the canopy that night.

. . . the tree is felled, decay sets in, and the pith rots away. But there remains an urge to live . . . a new generation springs up in its place.

George Nakashima

Do your part.

Do your part
of the world's suffering today.

Do your part
of the world's suffering today,
and I will do mine.

Do your part
of the world's suffering today,
and I will do mine
tomorrow.

Although the world is full of suffering, it is also full of the over-coming of it.

Helen Keller

Our dog, Bacchus, is contained in the yard by an underground electric fence. He will miss a whole day of adventuring in the world outside of his invisible boundaries because he is unwilling to subject himself to one second of pain. Silly Bacchus—we may cease considering you "man's best friend" if you remind us too much of the shocking reality of our own unrealized potential!

We know we live in a world full of suffering. Yet we are most comfortable when the suffering of the world is done by others—the ones we read about daily in the newspaper, the ones in the hospitals, the ones who live in countries burdened by war or hunger. Until suffering barges into our quiet lives unannounced, we live with what psychotherapist Irvin Yalom calls an "illusion of protection." We know that bad things happen to other people, but we believe that we are somehow immune.

Having the courage to embrace our own suffering brings freedom and growth. Failure can spring us loose from the grips of perfectionism or the delusion of superiority. Being wounded can make us balm for others' wounds. Grieving can transform our view of death. Bitterness deeply felt can eat its way through to forgiveness.

Holiness is a greater ideal by far than happiness because it embraces struggle.

David Wolpe

I can see your soul.

I can see your soul
is grand.

I can see your soul
is Grand
Canyon deep.

I can see your soul
is Grand
Canyon deep—
an awesome gorge.

I can see your soul
is Grand
Canyon deep—
an awesome, gorge-
ous, ancient spirit.

I remember a family vacation during which Dad, in his constant search for puns, proclaimed at the edge of Yellowstone Canyon: "By George, that gorge is gorgeous!"

Twenty-five years later, Claudia and I and the children took a three-week camping trip to Zion, Bryce, Grand Canyon, Grand Tetons, and Yellowstone National Parks. Sometime midway in the trip, after we'd seen the wonders of the first three parks, Claudia and I asked our children—then ages 2, 4, and 6—what part of the trip they had enjoyed the most. They all agreed that the cookies-and-cream milkshakes we'd had at a restaurant two nights before were easily the most spectacular highlight of the trip!

Young children can't fully appreciate the beauty of a scene like the Grand Canyon. Likewise, we adults often don't appreciate the beauty of our inner landscapes, especially the places where life has worn us down, the deep canyons where we've been wounded, the ones in which pride has been eroded and humility, humanness, and wisdom have been left behind.

If there be anywhere on earth a lover of God who is always kept safe from falling, I know nothing of it—for it was not shown me. But this was shown—that in falling and rising again we are always kept in the same precious love.

Julian of Norwich

I have become an empty shell.

I have become an empty shell,
a hermit.

I have become an empty shell.
A hermit
crab crawls inside.

I have become an empty shell.
A hermit
crab crawls inside
and calls me home.

One morning while vacationing in Florida, we packed everyone into the van and made the two-hour trip from Sarasota to Sanibel Island. On the ride there we told the kids about a spectacular bird sanctuary on Sanibel called Ding Darling, only to learn when we arrived that the preserve was closed for road construction.

Trying to salvage the trip, we decided to go shelling. Someone had told us about a beach where the sand dollars were so thick you couldn't keep from trampling them. The kids were excited again. We arrived and found nothing but a few broken shells. There wasn't a sand dollar in sight! We did see lots of crabs scurrying around on the beach, but they weren't what we came for.

Shortly after we returned home, Claudia and I were having a difficult morning. My lingering low spirits, complicated by Dad's pending death, had taken a toll on our usual closeness. She went to the park to get some space to reflect on it all.

Claudia composed the first and last lines of "I have become an empty shell," and I supplied the remaining lines. I'm proud of this collaborative effort, even moreso of our partnership through the joys and sorrows of the life we've made together.

Your pain is the breaking of the shell that encloses your understanding.

Kahlil Gibran

Death

A pious caterpillar believes.

A pious caterpillar believes,
an enlightened caterpillar knows.

A pious caterpillar believes.
An enlightened caterpillar knows
the winged life.

A pious caterpillar believes.
An enlightened caterpillar knows
the winged life
requires metamorphosis.

Who knows what beautiful and winged life . . . may unex-
pectedly come forth . . . to enjoy its perfect summer life at last!

Henry David Thoreau

Several years ago, one of our children found a cocoon during winter. We put it in a quart jar and placed it on top of the refrigerator. Gradually pushed back and out of sight, we found the jar months later. A luna moth filled it, all dead and dried and denied a chance to try its wings.

It may feel comfortable to live within the confines of our lives as we have currently constructed them, yet this can also cause us to suffocate spiritually, to miss the chance to live the winged life. We too often live with an unenlightened caterpillar consciousness, unable to imagine what there is beyond inching along and munching on the leaves of our routine lives. When a period of transformation is upon us, we'd sometimes rather go back to a familiar life than allow our crawling selves to die so that a winged life we know only dimly, if at all, can be born. Though our minds fear change, our souls know that transformation through darkness is a necessary part of the path to light.

The greatest transformation is, of course, death. What awaits is surely as unimaginable to us as the world of floating and fluttering is to a caterpillar.

I am living my dream.

I am living my dream
life with my dream woman.

I am living my dream
life with my dream woman
in my dream house.

I am living my dream
life with my dream woman
in my dream house,
forgetting that death will wake me.

We forget about death most of the time, which puts us to sleep at the wheel of our lives. We live most of the time as if this earthly existence is all there is. Consumed with the tasks of securing comforts for our bodies, we allow our souls to flicker weakly like candles drowning in their own wax.

If this life is truly only a brief chapter of our eternal stories—if, as I've heard it said, we are not human beings trying to be spiritual but spiritual beings trying to be human—then perhaps we *are* living a dream of sorts.

Imagine waking up someday and telling your celestial friends: "I had a dream about a strange and wonderful place called Earth. Everyone there lived in something called a 'body,' and there were two types of bodies—"male" and "female." To stay alive, you had to keep putting the remains of other creatures into a hole in your body called a 'mouth.' And you could make other beings like yourself called 'children.' As the dream went on, for years it seemed, there was an intense mixture of love and fear. It was a beautiful and difficult dream, and the only way for it to end was to let go by allowing the body to die."

Imagine your friends nodding knowingly, then embracing your spirit and saying, "Welcome home!"

Eternity is not something that begins after you are dead. It is going on all the time. We are in it now.

Charlotte Perkins Gilman

How can this suffering be?

How can this suffering be
a gift?

How can this suffering be
a gift?
Rip it open.

How can this suffering be
a gift?
Rip it open
and the heart floods with compassion.

The day Dad decided, by refusing dialysis, that it was his time to die, my brother Bob and I embraced and wept in the hallway outside his hospital room. We didn't intend to make a public display of it, but there was no private place to let the finality of Dad's decision sink in.

As we hugged, I asked Bob: "Why all the suffering? What's the point of a good man like Dad or anyone going through this?"

"I feel Dad is giving us a gift," Bob said, "the gift of compassion."

Though it was a gift I would happily have stamped "return to sender," I realized in time that Bob's insight was profound. We cannot be truly present with others in their pain until we have faced our own and become what Henri Nouwen called "wounded healers."

Unto a broken heart
No other one may go
Without the high perogative
Itself hath suffered too.

Emily Dickinson

Are you dying?

Are you dying
before my very eyes?

Are you dying
before my very eyes,
beloved father?

Are you dying?
Before my very eyes,
beloved father,
I see the face of God.

To love another person is to see the face of God.

Victor Hugo

When Dad decided to come home from the hospital to die, we were told that he had perhaps one to two days of lucidity left before the toxins in his blood would build up and put him in a coma. My sister Christy suggested that we have a "living funeral" while he was still of clear mind. For almost three hours we sang, prayed and talked heart-to-heart with him. When it was over, he said it was the happiest day of his life.

As we kept vigil with Dad for the next three days, we sang with him for hours. This seemed to be calming to him as he slipped away from us.

Mom asked me to sing at Dad's funeral. I wasn't at all sure that it was wise to agree to it. While I knew that a little choking up would be fine, it felt as if I might wretch violently in front of five hundred people. I wanted to sing the final song in *Les Miserables*, the one in which Jean Valjean and Cosette sing the well-known Victor Hugo line while Valjean is on his deathbed. When the chords proved too difficult for my guitar skills, I chose a song I'd written for Dad years earlier. His spirit must have been with me because my voice was strong and true.

Every time I look at his picture, I see the face of God and feel a surge of the deep longing that is our connection to the Great Spirit.

I'm slipping, my love.

I'm slipping, my love,
into something more comfortable.

I'm slipping, my love,
into something more comfortable,
and we'll make love again.

I'm slipping, my love,
into something more comfortable,
and we'll make love again
one day, perhaps, in the Great Beyond.

I wrote "I'm slipping, my love" as I watched my father sleep in a hospital room a week or so before he died. He was hooked up to an oxygen mask, a catheter, intravenous lines, and a feeding tube that was threaded down his nose—not a setting one would expect to inspire a meditation on erotic love.

One of the hardest things in life is to watch a loved one suffer and be able to do nothing about it. Because no doctor had yet pronounced Dad terminal, we held out hope for his recovery. Yet, as I sat in that darkened room, I hoped that he indeed was slipping out of his body into something more comfortable. I thought of his nearly fifty years of marriage to my mother and of the eight children that resulted from their passion for each other and for family life. I wondered if there is sex in the hereafter. If not, I decided, God had better have some other good ideas, because eternity is a long time to sit around just singing songs of praise and clanging cymbals!

One of the strange things about living in the world is that it is only now and then one is quite sure one is going to live for ever and ever and ever.

Frances Hodgson Burnett

This time of trial is long.

This time of trial is longing—patient, prayerful longing.

This time of trial is longing—patient, prayerful longing
for my healing into life or death.

This time of trial is longing—patient, prayerful longing—
for my healing into life or death
is in your hands alone, my God.

This time of trial is longing—patient, prayerful longing—
for my healing into life or death
is in your hands. Alone, my God,
I shall never be, for you enfold me always in your love.

For months before Dad died, I shared prayer several times per week with my parents. These prayer sessions were the only times Dad would say much about what was going on inside of him as he pondered the nearness of death. During them he stated how, despite his suffering, he felt enfolded in God's love. That word, "enfolded," came up repeatedly in his spontaneous prayer. I decided to incorporate "enfold" into the final line of "This time of trial is long," which I gave to Dad on Christmas Day. He died a month later.

It wasn't until a few months after his passing that I read some of David Bohm's *Wholeness and the Implicate Order,* one of Dad's favorite books. In that treatise, Bohm, an internationally-renowned physicist, discusses his observation that the reality of the whole universe is enfolded into even the smallest elements of the universe. The whole is represented in the structure of the parts.

In stating that he knew he was "enfolded" in God's love, Dad was making both a simple, almost childlike statement of faith and a sophisticated testament to his belief in how the universe is structured. My own faith has increased of necessity since his death. I have suspended the scientific objectivity with which I used to think about the afterlife. It isn't a question of science or even of whether or not the afterlife exists. Rather, it's a question of what manner of thinking will allow me to live this life with hope and anticipation rather than with grim resignation to suffering, death, and despair.

One cannot help but be in awe when he contemplates the mysteries of eternity, of life, of the marvelous structure of reality.

Albert Einstein

When you're gone I'll be in mourning.

When you're gone I'll be in mourning
doves' voices.

When you're gone I'll be in mourning
doves' voices
calling from beyond the screen.

When you're gone I'll be in mourning
doves' voices
calling from beyond the screen:
"I miss you you you."

Blessed are they who mourn, for they will be comforted.

Jesus of Nazareth

Birds were one of Dad's passions. After he died, I could not hear a mourning dove without being reminded of the grief, without feeling a deep "I miss you you you" in my soul. That was fine for a time, but I eventually decided to rewrite the piece, shifting the perspective to the other side of the screen that separates this life and the next:

When I'm gone I'll be in mourning.

When I'm gone I'll be in mourning
doves' voices.

When I'm gone I'll be in mourning
doves' voices
calling from beyond the screen.

When I'm gone I'll be in mourning
doves' voices
calling from beyond the screen:
"I'm with you you you."

Death leaves us cold.

Death leaves us cold
in the ground.

Death leaves us cold
in the ground
unless we burn.

Death leaves us cold
in the ground
unless we burn
on bright beyond the grave.

I was privileged to be present when Dad made his decision to allow his body to die. My sister Christy, Mom, and I were talking with the doctors, still hoping that dialysis would give Dad a chance of returning to some quality of life. What a dramatic shift it was when, after the doctor said that dialysis likely would not improve his condition and could introduce further complications, Dad said, "Take me home." We knew instantly what that meant.

Minutes later I heard my mother ask him if he wanted to be cremated. What a profound moment in the life of a marriage! One doesn't think about such questions in youth when the first flames of passion ignite. Dad said no to cremation because he thought the grandchildren would like to see his body.

I remember the cold firmness of his skin when I kissed his forehead just before they closed the casket. I knew he wasn't there, but his body was still a sacred reminder of the man I loved, and a kiss seemed the best way to say goodbye.

Death be not proud, though some have called thee
Mighty and dreadful, for thou art not so,
For those whom thou think'st thou dost overthrow
Die not, poor death, nor yet canst thou kill me . . .
One short sleep past, we wake eternally,
And death shall be no more; death, thou shalt die.

John Donne

Grief is a well.

Grief is a well-
worn sweater.

Grief is a well-
worn sweater
resting in the same closet still.

Grief is a well-
worn sweater
resting in the same closet, still
smelling like you.

When Dad returned from the hospital for his final days at home, he told us there were two things he wanted to live to see: his unborn grandson Jacob and the dogwood trees blooming in spring. Because dogwoods put out their buds in the fall, he told us, they would be marvelous in the spring. "They're loaded!" he said in a slurred voice. It was hard to hear him talk about his fondness for the dogwoods because spring was three months away, and we knew he had more like three *days* to live. Jacob shared his beauty with the world a few days after Dad's funeral. The dogwoods took the full three months to share theirs.

Dad was right—they were loaded! It was chillier than I expected the evening we gathered to celebrate the dogwoods. I went back into Mom and Dad's bedroom to find a sweater. Instead I found a sacred reminder of the man we had gathered to celebrate. The many ordinary possessions a person leaves behind suddenly take on great significance when death carves a hollow in our hearts. A deceased loved one's garments seem to be among the reminders that lead us most quickly back to the well of grief.

Grief is such a holy longing. Our lives here are transformed by it into a blessed unfinishedness. The great cosmic question of the afterlife becomes personal. We now have business on the other side. In grief we experience a longing for reunion with our loved ones, which we sense is one with our longing for reunion with God.

When you are sorrowful look again in your heart, and you shall see that in truth you are weeping for that which has been your delight.

Kahlil Gibran

All I want is to create.

All I want is to create
of my life a singular crystalline structure.

All I want is to create
of my life a singular crystalline structure—
falling

        falling

                falling.

All I want is to create
of my life a singular crystalline structure—
falling

        falling

                falling
toward the outstretched tongue of God.

Who seeing the snowflake . . . can fail to entertain a central thought: . . . that we are the natural expressions of a deeper order.

Stuart Kauffman

A few years ago, a friend and I made a fire and sat by a creek on an overcast, chilly March afternoon. The prior autumn's leaves still carpeted the woods. As we talked, we suddenly heard a strange tapping sound. All around us, tiny pieces of ice were falling from the sky, making tympanic membranes of the dead leaves. Upon closer inspection, each piece of ice was formed in the perfect shape of a Star of David. I'd never seen anything like it and haven't since. What amazements the natural world can spring on us!

Our journey is not unlike that of a snowflake which starts as water taken up by and held imperceptibly in air, becomes visible as a unique and intricate crystalline form, and falls briefly and beautifully before melting back to its original state.

A drop of water remains a drop of water whether it falls from the sky as a flake or a star, or spills from an eye, or frosts a blade of grass, or flows with the current of a mountain stream, or circulates through your bloodstream, or pulsates with the ocean tide, or obscures the sun on a foggy morning. Perhaps if we could believe that, like water, the Divine energy that is our essence can exist in many forms, we would not cling so desperately to youth and avoid anything that reminds us of the melting we call death.

My life is a gestation.

My life is a gestation,
this world is but a womb.

My life is a gestation,
this world is but a womb,
death's another birth.

My life is a gestation,
this world is but a womb,
death's another birth
canal, and dying's just hard labor.

I think of death as some delightful journey
that I shall take when all my tasks are done.

Ella Wheeler Wilcox

"Aren't you afraid to die?" my sister asked Dad just after his decision at the hospital. "I find it so enticing!" he replied.

Writing "My life is a gestation" helped clarify my thoughts about death. Before seeing death up close, I held an agnostic attitude about the afterlife: maybe we live on, maybe we don't. I didn't realize that maintaining a neutral stance was actually allowing my soul to fill up with fear. I thought I was on fire with life, but I wasn't aware that fear—the shadow of love—was beginning to choke my soul with its black smoke.

Dad's year of suffering following poisoning by a medication caused me even greater existential angst. *How could a thing like this happen to such a good man?* I thought. "Don't try to figure out suffering, Kev—it will drive you crazy," Dad told me during one of our prayer sessions in the months before he died.

None of us will ever solve the mystery of suffering and death. But now I choose to think of dying as just hard labor.

Longing, Fear, and Hope

I like you.

I, like you,
long to have it all.

I, like you,
long to have it all
mean something.

I, like you,
long to have it all
mean something
when I'm gone.

I've asked hundreds of people in psychotherapy what they consider to be the purpose of life. The most frequent response I've received is: "I'm like everybody else—I just want to have it all."

A few years ago I wrote a song titled "We All Have It All." When most of us say we want it all, what we really mean is we want all the *good* things in life—success, wealth, a happy family. It's as if we want to play a magnificent piano concerto while avoiding all the dark keys. In reality, we all have it all. Each of our lives is a mixture of success and failure. Our relationships contain joy and pain. We all have both routine and peak experiences.

Our longing to be filled up with material things is a reflection of a much deeper desire to experience infinite abundance. When we recognize that acquisitiveness is driven by longing for the Infinite and that this life will never satisfy that longing, we free ourselves to accept the mix of joy and pain that plays out in our lives and the lives of everyone else on the planet. We also become more capable of channeling our longing to its Source, which transforms our days into lived prayers.

One has seen but half the universe who has never been shown the house of pain.

Ralph Waldo Emerson

Do you still drink too much?

Do you still drink too much
from the well of longing?

Do you still drink too much
from the well of longing
for what you haven't yet?

Do you still drink too much
from the well of longing
for what you haven't yet
transcended?

Half of the spiritual material I read emphasizes living life with passion; the other half addresses the importance of transcending the passions of this world which only keep us from growing spiritually. No wonder I'm confused!

As a theologian friend of mine says, we are finite creatures with infinite longings. In pursuing the pleasures of this world, we may discover some of the ecstatic energy of the Creator. We also risk creating false idols and addictions. Aristotle seemed to have it right when he encouraged striving for the golden mean between extremes. Yet Jesus was not one to encourage moderation in the spiritual life, saying God would spit the lukewarm out of his mouth. How easy it is to be conflicted about what to do with our human longings!

Perhaps wisdom involves both loving life passionately and cultivating a detachment that allows us to avoid clinging to the pleasures of this world, for we are only visitors here.

To be without some of the things you want is an indispensable part of happiness.

Bertrand Russell

The river is still.

The river is still
longing for rain.

The river is still
longing for rain-
swelled clouds to come.

The river is still
longing for rain-
swelled clouds to come
with her and make her wild again.

In wildness is the preservation of the world.

Henry David Thoreau

One particularly arid summer, the scenic creek behind our home completely dried up. Dead clams and fish were scattered among the rocks. We gathered wood, made a fire, and roasted hot dogs right there in the middle of the creek bed. Our children giggled as they watched a pair of groundhogs mate a short distance away on the bare bedrock.

There was something magical about sitting in a spot so exposed— a place which nature normally covers in a flowing robe of wetness. Relaxing there on a sweltering summer afternoon, watching flies buzz about the casualties of drought, I sensed that all the wild creatures in this ecological system, even the creek bed herself, were longing for rain. The scene was hot, sultry—charged, to paraphrase Gerard Manley Hopkins, with the eros of God.

Just as nature is suffused with God's creative and erotic power, each human being pulsates with a mysterious sexual energy—a longing for the ecstatic, a deep desire to know wildness again.

153

Fear is a weed.

Fear is a weed
I pull up again and again.

Fear is a weed
I pull up. Again and again
it chokes the garden of my joy.

Fear is a weed
I pull up. Again and again
it chokes the garden of my joy.
I just don't get it!

Fear is a weed
I pull up. Again and again
it chokes the garden of my joy.
I just don't get it
by the roots.

Fear defeats more people than any other one thing in the world.

Ralph Waldo Emerson

While he was ill and I was in angst, Dad recommended I read *Molecules of Emotion* by Candice Pert. In this fascinating book, Pert lays out the evidence that our minds, emotions, and bodies are intricately intertwined. On a physical level, our emotions translate instantaneously into chemical changes in the body that can produce states of well-being or pain. The system, according to Pert, does not work in a top-down way, with only the brain determining what is felt in the emotions or in the body. Rather, cells throughout our bodies release hundreds of different peptides and neurotransmitters that we experience as emotions or physical sensations. If we doubt this mind-emotion-body connection, we need only think of the blushing that follows embarrassment or the urge to go to the bathroom that accompanies anxiety to realize how integrated we are.

Fear—along with depression, anger, resentment and similar negative emotions—makes our bodies release substances that poison joy and damage health. Fear is also what motivates most of the hatred in the world. Living for ultimate concerns, instead of being embedded in anxiety about our own narrow interests, loosens the soil around our fears and allows us to begin getting them by the roots.

I knelt beside your bed last night.

I knelt beside your bed last night,
feeling you constantly while your fever broke.

I knelt beside your bed last night,
feeling you constantly while your fever broke
open the places I've been hiding.

I knelt beside your bed last night,
feeling you constantly while your fever broke
open the places I've been hiding
my darkest fears.

One night while camping with the family in Pennsylvania, I awoke at 3:00 a.m. to the sound of two raccoons climbing across the top of our van. To my dismay, I discovered that one of the van windows had been left open, and there were two more raccoons feasting inside on the food we had stored there for safekeeping.

A day after returning from the trip, our then two-year-old son, Jim, became ill with a high fever and diarrhea. These symptoms went on for a month, and the doctors could not figure out what the problem was. Having heard that raccoons carry a roundworm that can be fatal to humans, I became convinced that Jim had it. That summer I prayed beside his bed many nights into the early hours of the morning.

There's a thin line between love and fear. The more we love, the more fear can try to infect our souls. When we love, we open ourselves to joy and pain, hope and fear—the whole light and dark keyboard of human emotions.

I've heard it said that the only cure for fear is faith. But I must admit, I often wonder why the next world is so veiled in mystery. Why the big secret, God? In the end, such questions don't get us very far. Cultivating acceptance, hope, love, and faith leads to a far richer experience of this mystery we call life than permitting fear to run amok in our souls.

Your children are not your children.
They are sons and daughters
of life's longing for itself.

Kahlil Gibran

Fear is a patient preyer.

Fear is a patient preyer
waiting always unseen in the shadows.

Fear is a patient preyer
waiting always unseen in the shadows
for those who fall.

Fear is a patient preyer
waiting always unseen in the shadows
for those who fall
into sickness or despair.

Hope is a patient prayer.

Hope is a patient prayer
waiting always unseen in the shadows.

Hope is a patient prayer
waiting always unseen in the shadows
for those who fall.

Hope is a patient prayer
waiting always unseen in the shadows
for those who fall
into sickness or despair.

Tell me, how can I not believe?

Tell me, how can I not believe
in the next world?

Tell me, how can I not believe
in the next world,
having experienced this one?

Tell me, how can I not believe
in the next world,
having experienced this one
to be so unbelievable?

Our faith comes in moments, yet there is a depth in those brief moments which constrains us to ascribe more reality to them than to all other experiences.

Ralph Waldo Emerson

One morning I looked at the scene outside our bedroom window and the phrase, *How can I not believe in the next world?* came spontaneously into my mind. The entire landscape—every branch, every blade of grass—was coated with crystals created when cool air transformed the fog that had blanketed us the night before. It was one of those exquisitely beautiful scenes that has the power to jolt us out of ordinary consciousness into a sense of how inconceivable life is, how amazing it is that we are here at all.

And if we are here, why could we not also find ourselves somewhere else after we leave this world? Would the existence of life after death be any more surprising than the reality of life before death?

Joy

I like you.

I, like you,
have many routine days.

I, like you,
have many routine days
and moments.

I, like you,
have many routine days
and moments
of sheer joy.

An "epiphany" is a moment when life breaks through to us. We can experience such moments regularly only if we keep attuned to the deep possibilities of seemingly ordinary events.

One of the most memorable epiphanies I have experienced occurred three years ago. The whole family was riding bicycles on a trail through a forest during autumn when six-year-old Lizzie announced that she would catch a falling leaf in her mouth while riding her bike. Briefly intrigued by her declared intention, I tried it for five minutes or so. After deeming that it was too difficult and might lead me to chase a falling leaf right into the trunk of a tree, I resumed simply enjoying the ride. For the next hour, however, Lizzie pedaled behind me with her mouth open, keeping herself prepared in every moment for the catch. Periodically she called out, "My throat is getting so-o-o dry!" but the mouth stayed open.

Then, in a glorious burst of childhood exuberance, Lizzie screamed by me on her bike, managing to hold a golden leaf secure in her teeth while shouting, "I got it! I got it!" I tried to catch that sacred moment, lived fully in a flash of joy, and hold on to it. But as I watched her ride away, I felt it slip through my fingers and land somewhere on the path behind me.

Did you ever observe to whom accidents happen? Chance favors only the prepared mind.

Louis Pasteur

Be still.

Be still
surprised.

Be still
surprised
by the day today.

Be still
surprised
by the day-to-day
miracles.

As for me, I know of nothing else but miracles.

Walt Whitman

The invariable mark of wisdom is to see the miraculous in the common.

Ralph Waldo Emerson

There are two ways to live your life. One is as though nothing is a miracle. The other is as though everything is a miracle.

Albert Einstein

When I was born I was so surprised I couldn't talk for a year and a half.

Gracie Allen

To have faith that our lives are indeed eternal, our minds long for supernatural miracles. Yet we are permeated by the miraculous like pickles in brine. Every time we breathe or have a thought or laugh or make love or experience countless other ordinary events of life, we participate in the miraculous.

I don't know.

I don't know
about life after death.

I don't know
about life after death,
but daily I make the choice to believe.

I don't know
about life after death,
but daily I make the choice to believe
passionately in life before death.

The sense of this word among the Greeks affords the noblest definition of it; "enthusiasm" signifies "God in us."

Mme. Ann de Stael

Even more than "enthusiasm," I like the word "passion" because it has at least three distinct meanings. First, passion of a sexual nature is "God in us" in the desire to merge with our beloved and in the power to create life. Second, if we live with passion we experience "God in us" as we respond to the Divine energies that flow in our souls. Such passion motivates us to go through our days with a sense of celebration, depth, and purpose. Lastly, in this life we experience passion as Jesus did in his final days of suffering and execution. Our sufferings are not caused by God, but we can experience "God in us" through them if we stop judging them and accept their invitation to grow.

Let's eat out.

Let's eat out-
side tonight.

Let's eat out-
side. Tonight
could be our last together.

Let's eat out-
side. Tonight
could be our last. Together
let us lift our goblets to the stars!

I went to the woods because I wished to live deliberately, to front only the essential facts of life, and see if I could not learn what it had to teach, and not, when I came to die, discover that I had not lived . . . I wanted to live deep and suck out all the marrow of life.

Henry David Thoreau

As a boy, I remember how Dad used to chomp through chicken bones at dinner and suck the marrow out of them. He claimed it was the best part. That's how he lived, too. Though he was seventy-six when he died and had been ill for a year, I experienced his leaving us as sudden and unexpected. I had no idea when the new millennium came in that the year 2000 would be our last with him as a healthy man.

How is it that this year after my father's death has been the most joyful of my life? I think it is because the longing for him is never far from my consciousness. His death has embedded Death on my daily awareness, and the result has been joy. Carrying the memory of a person like that in one's heart is a constant reminder to live with passion.

The last thing anyone wants on his or her tombstone is *Died at 50, buried at 80.* Our culture shapes us to think death is the enemy of life, but the reverse is true. Daily awareness of death fans the fire of joy and spurs us to live deeply and deliberately.

Do you tend to live as if there is no time for joy? I did and still do at times. The truth is, there is no time *not* to live with joy.

Bluegills eat watermelon!

"Bluegills eat watermelon,
Dad!" he said, his spirit still sharp.

"Bluegills eat watermelon,
Dad!" he said, his spirit still sharp
as a fillet knife used for gutting.

"Bluegills eat watermelon,
Dad!" he said, his spirit still sharp
as a fillet knife used for gutting
the insidious lure of habituation.

*Genius . . . means little more than the faculty of perceiving in an
unhabitual way.*

William James

Can you imagine the ability to delight in learning that bluegills
eat watermelon, something our four-year-old son Jim discovered one
summer day after he ran out of worms? Can you imagine being the
bluegill, tired of eating whatever it is that bluegills eat every day, tast-
ing watermelon for the first time?

Our brains are wired to respond with "habituation" to anything
we are exposed to repeatedly—a dulling of our appreciation for what
formerly may have created joy and excitement. When we are children everything is a new discovery, and few things in our experience
have become habituated. Many adults experience most of life with a
habituated perception—a chronic, low-level boredom with the known
and the familiar.

Living with joy means eviscerating habituation. What if we woke
up every morning as if everything were new? "Wow, look—the sun's
coming up!" we'd say or, "There aren't enough O's in 'good' to describe this pizza!" or maybe even, "What an amazing privilege to be
spending my life with you!"

Joy is an infallible sign of the presence of God.

Pierre Teilhard de Chardin

Do you have the time?

Do you have the time
of your life?

Do you have the time
of your life
or does someone else perhaps?

Do you have the time
of your life
or does someone else? Perhaps
it's later than you think.

I remember hearing about a life insurance company that sells a clock into which you can program your gender, age, height, weight, and smoking status. With that information, the clock is able to estimate your life expectancy and begin ticking backward from your calculated date of departure from this world. Such a clock, I suppose, could either inspire us to greatness or drive us to despair!

Recently I was rollerblading along a bike trail near our home, lost in a meditative trance induced by the rhythm of the exercise and the music on the CD player. At one point, I raised both arms as if to conduct the symphony I was hearing through the headphones, which promptly threw off my balance and landed me hard in a heap on the pavement a half second later. That's how fast our lives can change. It's also how quickly death can take us.

Should we live in fear of this reality? What would be the point? We need to make our peace with our "only visiting" status in this life and decide to laugh and love and live "flat out" anyway, knowing full well that death can knock at any time.

All my possessions for a moment of time.

Last words of Elizabeth I, 1603

Joy is succulent, wild!

Joy is succulent, wild
black raspberries.

Joy is succulent, wild
black raspberries
overhanging every path.

Joy is succulent, wild
black raspberries
overhanging every path,
scratching for your attention right and left.

Joy is succulent, wild
black raspberries
overhanging every path,
scratching for your attention, right? And left
mostly unpicked?

Earth's crammed with heaven,
And every common bush afire with God.

Elizabeth Barrett Browning

My siblings and I still occasionally tease an older brother about a comment he made while we were backpacking through the Beartooth Range of the Rocky Mountains in Montana nearly twenty years ago. After a long uphill trek, several of us toward the front of the line of hikers had stopped to rest and pick some raspberries by the side of the trail. My brother was focused on making time and exhorted us to move on by shouting: "Cut the berries!"

Don't we too often cut the berries out of life? It's so easy to walk right on by, not even noticing their juicy ripeness because we are focused on getting somewhere else.

What robs us of joy in life? Busyness, focus on money, preoccupation with meeting unrealistic standards of beauty or accomplishment, neglect of relationships, comparison to others we think have it better than we do—all of these and more can cause us to walk right past the succulent fruit overhanging our own paths.

Black raspberries are picked by our bare hands and stain them purple; everyday joys are picked by our bared spirits and color them blessed.

Many years I waited.

Many years I waited
for bluebirds to show up.

Many years I waited
for bluebirds to show, up-
lifting me with their plumage.

Many years I waited.
For bluebirds to show, up-
lifting me with their plumage,
I had only to build them a home.

Several times I had been told that the five-acre parcel we live on is ideal for bluebird nesting. Yet, after seven years here, I was pretty sure there weren't a lot of extra bluebirds around waiting to grace our yard if I went to the trouble of putting a box up for them. Finally, on one of those aimless Saturdays, I decided to assemble and put up a bluebird box just thirty feet from the back of our home. *Probably too close for them to nest here*, I thought. But the next day, there they were—a male and female looking for a place to raise a clutch together.

All that spring and summer as I saw that pair come and go, their blues brought me joy. Somehow their presence made me feel like the scene in *Bambi*, just after the hero learns that his mother has been killed. Disney can do a lot to raise your spirits with some animated, chirping birds and a catchy tune. These real-life birds seemed to arrive in my world to do the same for me just a few months after Dad left.

What amazed me about their arrival was how they showed up the very day after I built a home for them. I don't think it was luck. They were there all along, I think, hiding in the trees, invisible to one not looking closely for them. I wonder how many joys are like that—just waiting for us to build them a home.

> *For those leaning on the sustaining infinite,*
> *today is big with blessings.*
>
> Mary Baker Eddy

I have known joy.

I have known joy
in this world.

I have known joy
in this world
like a blossoming.

I have known joy
in this world
like a blossoming
flower knows butterflies.

Earth laughs in flowers.

Ralph Waldo Emerson

APPENDIX:
WHAT IS A NESTED MEDITATION?

I have chosen to call the pieces in this volume nested meditations rather than poems. The verse in *Divinity in Disguise* is out of step with modern poetry in several ways. First, it is subject to certain structural rules, on which I will elaborate shortly. Robert Frost once said that writing in free verse (no rhyme or meter) is like "playing tennis without a net." He felt that the demands of structure improved his poetry. Most modern poets, however, prefer to write with no net because it gives complete freedom to create without rules.

Second, nested meditations are meant to be highly accessible—short and understandable upon first reading, though rich enough to invite repeated readings. Modern poetry is often inaccessible to the average reader, either because the poems are difficult to comprehend even with repeated readings or because their length discourages all but poetry enthusiasts.

Third, while good poetry generally avoids the use of clichés or idioms, the nested form sometimes uses them to set up an expectation in the reader's mind, only to change and deepen the meaning of the piece as later lines are added.

Fourth, nested meditations use wordplay that would be considered appropriate only in "light" or humorous verse by most poetry critics. However, the use of wordplay in nested verse is usually not intended for humor. Rather, it is meant to surprise the mind with a new and unexpected image or thought.

Finally, most poems, even modern ones, have titles. Just as Emily Dickinson, however, did not give titles to her brief poems, I have chosen to forego giving titles to these meditations. This is because much of the enjoyment of a nested meditation is in the shifting meaning of the piece as it unfolds, which requires that the reader have no prior knowledge of the themes present in the meditation. In most cases a title would serve to spoil the surprise.

So what is a nested meditation? It is easiest to describe this form by considering an example:

> I picked you.
>
> I picked you
> to be my wife.
>
> I picked you
> to be my wife
> and I didn't know you.
>
> I picked you
> to be my wife
> and I didn't know you
> were a wildflower.

The piece is called "nested" because each stanza contains the previous stanza and adds a single line that usually changes the meaning of the piece.

The goal of a nested meditation is to let each stanza stand alone as its own statement or meditation. In "I picked you," the second stanza is a simple statement: *I picked you / to be my wife.*

The third stanza addresses the reality that when we choose to marry someone, we really don't know him or her as well as we think, though we're convinced that we do. The fourth line in the final stanza (*were a wildflower*) both conveys the beauty of the beloved and sheds new light on the first line (*I picked you*). As in this example, some nested meditations have a circular quality. That is, after reading the entire piece, the reader can circle back to earlier lines and find new meaning in them.

The rules for writing nested meditations are as follows:

1. The piece begins with a single line which forms a complete sentence.
2. Each succeeding stanza contains the previous line or lines and adds one new line.
3. Each stanza forms its own grammatically correct, complete sentence (or, in some cases, more than one sentence).
4. No words in previous lines of the piece can be changed, with the exception that a word can be capitalized or uncapitalized. The order and spelling of words cannot be changed. (I have violated this rule twice. In "Help me!" the spelling of "damn" changes to "dam," and in "My wife is my home" the word "raise" becomes "raze.")
5. Punctuation changes in previous lines are allowed. This includes the addition or removal of hyphens, commas, periods or other punctuation. In this form, altering punctuation is one of the main devices for altering meaning.

The nested meditation seems most similar in its intent to a familiar form of poetic expression, the haiku. In three lines, a haiku aims to capture the pristine beauty of a moment. The language is simple and fresh, intending to draw the reader into an experience of the moment as the writer felt it move her or him to words. Though longer than the haiku, the nested meditation likewise follows a brief and simple structure and is intended as a succinct expression of an aspect of life as the writer has experienced it.

The reader is encouraged to try writing his or her own nested meditations. I suggest this because I have found that the writing of these pieces often reveals something new to me about myself or about life. Frequently I am surprised by the words as they appear on the page. One begins with a single line and follows the piece where it goes, learning about oneself and life in the process. My hope is that any quiet enjoyment you experience in the pieces I have written will inspire you to further reflection through the writing of your own nested meditations.

Alphabetical Index of First Lines

A Word About Ralph Waldo Emerson

In searching for quotations to accompany the nested meditations, I found myself drawn consistently to Emerson's wisdom and poetic way with words. At first, seeing that Emerson's quotes outnumbered the next-closest person by five to one, I thought of replacing some of his quotes to include a broader array of others. Eventually, I decided to simply allow and welcome his contribution to this work.

Becoming better acquainted with Emerson's writings has been a bonus for the effort put into creating this book.

For those not familiar with the life and writings of this great American, Robert Richardson's *Emerson: A Mind on Fire* serves as a compelling biographical introduction.

Original Emerson quotations presented in gender-neutral language in the text:

Every man is a divinity in disguise . . . (p. 19)

Man is a stream whose source is hidden. Our being is descending into us from we know not whence. (p. 31)

Men cease to interest us when we find their limitations. (p. 23)

As long as a man stands in his own way, everything seems to be in his way. (p. 79)

He has seen but half the universe who has never been shown the house of pain. (p. 149)

To order additional copies of *Divinity in Disguise*:

Number of copies desired: _____

Subtotal ($19.95 per book): $_____

Add 6.25% sales tax for orders shipped to Ohio addresses:

Sales Tax $_____

Add $2.95 shipping and handling for the first book and $1.95 for each additional book.

Shipping and handling: $_____

Total: $_____

Payment: ___ Check ___ Money order
Payable to: Center for Life Balance

Ship to:

Name: _____

Address: _____

City: _____

State: _____ Zip Code: _____

e-mail address: _____

Send this form when completed to:
Center for Life Balance
PO Box 74
Monclova, OH 43542

Allow four weeks for delivery.

For more information about Kevin Anderson's work, visit:

centerforlifebalance.net

or write to:

Center for Life Balance
PO Box 74
Monclova, OH 43542